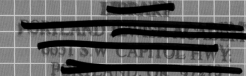

Washington D.C.

science QUEST

An Invisible Force

The Quest to Define the Laws of Motion

Glen Phelan

The Mad Tea Party Ride at Disneyland, illustrating the laws of motion

CONTENTS

The invention of the printing press in 1454 made books available to many people.

INTRODUCTION

Scientists on trial…threats of torture and death…a Great Plague sweeping the countryside. Sounds like a great story. Well, it is—and it's true! This is the story of people who dared to look at things in new ways. It's the story of how we came to understand how things move—on Earth and in space.

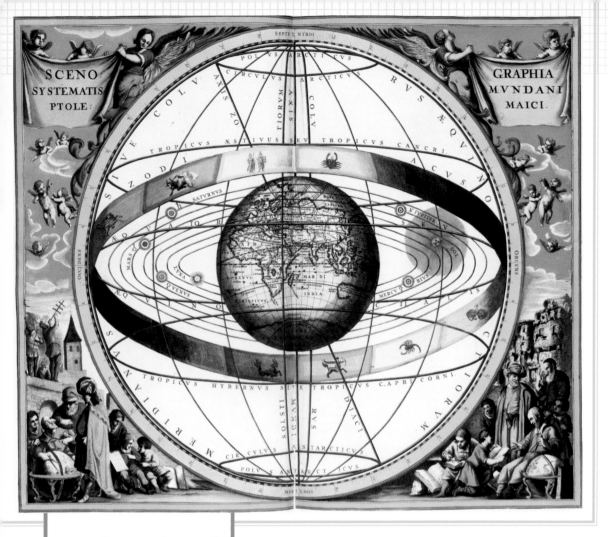

A seventh-century diagram of the universe with Earth shown at the center

Life During the Renaissance

The Renaissance was a time of great change in Europe. It lasted from the 1300s to the early 1600s. At the time, many people lived in or around castles. Cities grew. Explorers sailed across oceans and visited new lands. People exchanged goods and ideas. It was an Age of Discovery.

Much of Renaissance life in Europe was influenced by the Catholic Church—the main religious body in Europe at the time. Church leaders were as powerful as government leaders. And the Church expected people to strictly obey its rules and beliefs. If you did not, you were called a heretic and were generally faced with a court trial.

1454
First printing press
in Europe

A 14th-century astrolabe, used
to measure stars' positions

The court of the Church, called the Inquisition, was very
powerful. A person found guilty by the Inquisition could
end up in prison—or worse. Many heretics were burned
at the stake.

The Church had strong beliefs on many topics, including
how heavenly bodies (objects in the universe) moved.
Most people believed that Earth was the center of the
universe. It stood still while the sun, moon, planets, and
stars moved around it. That's what Ptolemy, a great
ancient thinker, had taught in the second century, and
the Church strictly enforced this view. Anyone who
thought otherwise would be considered a heretic.
However, in spite of the risks, someone would soon
come along to challenge this idea.

A 15th-century map of Europe based on the teachings of Ptolemy

STARGAZING & HERESY

In 1493, Nicolaus Copernicus found himself amazed. Christopher Columbus's discovery of new lands proved that the world was bigger than maps of the time showed. Nicolaus knew that the Greek philosopher Ptolemy had made those maps centuries before. If Ptolemy had made mistakes in his maps, Copernicus wondered, was he wrong about other things, too?

Nicolaus Copernicus

BORN February 19, 1473
Torun, Poland

DIED May 24, 1543
Frombork, Poland

As a little boy, Nicolaus loved learning the ancient Greek stories of the constellations so much that he learned them by heart.

As an adult, Copernicus became an astronomer and studied in Italy as well as his native country, Poland. Through his studies he became an expert in the math, medicine, astronomy, and theology of the times.

Often called the founder of modern astronomy, Copernicus changed science forever. He showed that the Earth turned on an axis once every day and that it circled the sun once every year. These two theories revolutionized science, and his model of the universe launched the Copernican Revolution.

1473

Nicolaus Copernicus is born.

As a child, Nicolaus liked to learn about the stars and the universe. As he grew older, he had many questions. Why were some stars brighter than others? Why were some planets next to certain stars on some nights and next to other stars on other nights? What were shooting stars, and where did they go?

Professors and church leaders depended on the writings of Aristotle, Ptolemy, and other ancient Greek thinkers for the answers. But Nicolaus always wondered.

While studying astronomy at a university in Cracow, Poland, Nicolaus was invited by an astronomy professor to use instruments that measured where stars and planets were. Nicolaus was thrilled. He would learn how to make star maps like Ptolemy's. The main instrument he would use was an astrolabe. He would line up a part of the astrolabe with a star to measure where it was in the sky. By using mathematics, he could then make a map of the sky on paper and place any star on the map.

A painting of astronomer and explorer Amerigo Vespucci using an astrolabe to make a star map

1492 Christopher Columbus arrives in the New World.

1500 The Inca empire flourishes.

science BOOSTER

Did You Know?
Claudius Ptolemy, born in Egypt around 85 A.D., was one of the most influential Greek astronomers, geographers, and mathematicians of his time. In memory of his incredible accomplishments, Ptolemy has both a moon crater and a Mars crater named after him.

An Old Idea

Nicolaus carefully measured the location of a star. Then he compared it to Ptolemy's star map. To his surprise, the positions were different. His professor agreed. He, too, had taken many measurements and found that the old star maps were often wrong. If those maps were wrong, did that mean Ptolemy's entire model of the universe—with Earth at the center—might be wrong, too?

Then the professor told Nicolaus about an old idea.

One Greek thinker had taught that Earth moves around the sun. This idea had been forgotten over the centuries. Nicolaus had never heard of this idea before, but now he couldn't get it out of his mind. The thought of Earth *moving* was fantastic!

In a way, it made a lot of sense. Nicolaus knew that motion can fool you. For instance, from a boat floating down a river, it seems that the shore is moving. Instead, the boat is moving. Maybe it was the same thing with Earth and the sun.

Copernicus lived in this castle in Lidzbark Warminski, Poland.

The Questions Continue

Later, Nicolaus served as an assistant to his uncle who was a bishop in Poland. From his bedroom in his uncle's castle, Nicolaus observed the stars and planets. He often kept notes about the planet Mars.

Usually, Mars seemed to move across the sky from west to east. Then it would seem to stand still. Then it seemed to back up and move from east to west. This pattern of movement happened over many months.

Magellan's crew circumnavigates the globe.

The ancient Greek philosopher Ptolemy had noticed it, too. He explained it by saying that as the planets moved around Earth, they also moved in little circles, as if they were being stirred. Nicolaus also noticed that Mars's brightness changed during the year, as if its distance from Earth changed. But if Mars moved around Earth in a circle, it would always be the same distance away. That means it would always have the same brightness. Nicolaus never quite believed the "stirring" explanation and wondered how there might be a different truth that explained these observations.

Putting Two and Two Together

Nicolaus thought about the mistakes in Ptolemy's maps. He thought about the long-forgotten idea that Earth might be the one moving. He thought about how motion can fool you. Then, he took a sheet of paper, dipped his pen in ink, and drew a new model of the universe.

Nicolaus's new model answered many questions. For example, why did Mars seem to back up in the sky? It could be that Earth was passing Mars along Earth's inner orbit. This would be like a runner on an inside lane passing a runner on an outside lane.

Copernicus publishes his
sun-centered theory.

Nicolaus Copernicus dies.

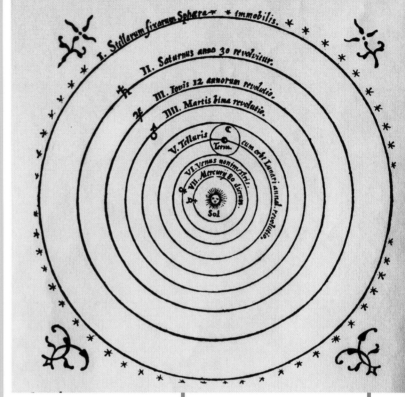

This diagram, drawn by
Copernicus, shows his model of
a sun-centered universe.

Nicolaus's drawing also explained day and night. Not only
did Earth move around the sun, but it rotated every 24
hours. This rotation made it seem as if the sun was moving
across the sky. We don't feel Earth's rotation because we
travel with Earth. It's like being on a large moving ship. If
the water is calm, you really don't feel like you're moving.

Over the next 30 years, Nicolaus Copernicus recorded
many more observations. They helped support his new
model of the universe. He published a book about it just
before he died in 1543. Copernicus showed how Earth
and the planets move in space. He also paved the way
for others who wondered about how things move.

Florence, the city where Galileo did much of his research on motion

PICKING UP THE PACE

Nicolaus Copernicus's model of the universe was well known only to a small group of scholars. And many of them thought it was nonsense. But 21 years after his death, a child was born who would grow up and pick up where Copernicus left off. Galileo Galilei would find the proof that Copernicus could not.

Did Galileo drop cannonballs? Here's one artist's view of what might have happened.

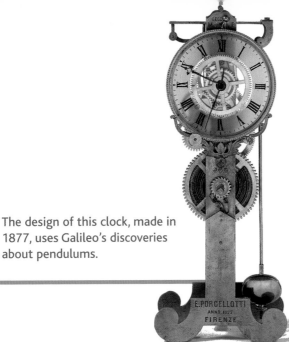

The design of this clock, made in 1877, uses Galileo's discoveries about pendulums.

Galileo Galilei

BORN February 15, 1564
Pisa, Tuscany

DIED January 8, 1642
near Florence, Tuscany

Galileo Galilei was a curious young boy. He took great care to observe the world around him. He was especially curious about how things moved—not just stars and planets. To satisfy his curiosity, Galileo did what very few people up to that time ever did. He experimented. And as a result—he discovered.

By the age of 25, Galileo had become a professor of mathematics at the University of Pisa. He developed the experimental method and changed the field of science forever.

One day, young Galileo was in church. He saw that a lamplighter had accidentally knocked a chandelier. The chandelier swung back and forth on its long chain, making an arc through the air. To anyone else who noticed, the swinging light was probably annoying. But to Galileo, it was an experiment.

As he watched the chandelier, the swings got smaller and smaller. Galileo measured the time of each swing with his pulse. (Reliable clocks and watches had not been invented yet.) To his surprise, the large swings took exactly the same amount of time as the small ones!

Galileo repeated this experiment many times. He used a weight hung on a chain. When the swing was large, the weight moved faster, so it took the same amount of time as the smaller swings. The smaller swings were slower. Galileo had discovered the law of the pendulum. He used this discovery to design a pendulum clock.

1564

Galileo Galilei is born.

1571

Johannes Kepler is born.

New Ideas, New Enemies

When he grew up, Galileo went to teach at the University of Pisa. There, he made another discovery. Most people believed that heavy objects fall faster than lighter ones. It made sense, and no one had tried to prove it. But Galileo thought that all objects would fall at the same speed.

There is a legend about how Galileo proved his point. He dropped a heavy cannonball and a lighter cannonball off the Leaning Tower of Pisa. The balls hit the ground at the same time. Galileo was right! No one knows if he really did this experiment from the tower. But we know that he did similar experiments rolling balls down a ramp.

You might think Galileo's experiments would have convinced everyone. But most other professors were not impressed. They still believed the old ideas. Galileo was annoyed. He criticized the professors for teaching things that were wrong. He made many enemies and was forced to leave the university.

> Most people believed that heavy objects fall faster than lighter ones.

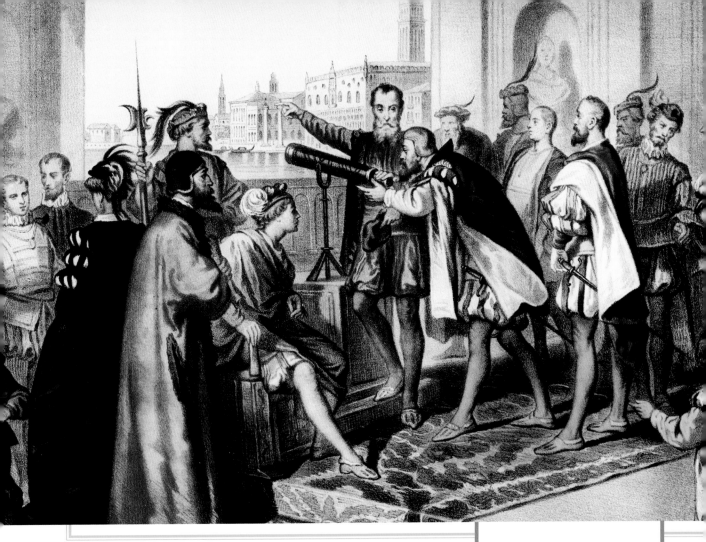

Seeing Farther

After leaving the university, Galileo moved to Padua in the Republic of Venice. Here, people accepted new ideas more easily. He thought a lot about how the stars and planets move. Galileo had read Copernicus's book and agreed with him that the sun must be the center of the universe. But there was no proof.

Then one day in 1609, Galileo heard that a Dutch lens grinder had invented a tool that made distant objects appear closer. It was called a spyglass. He sent for one right away.

1607

Colonists arrive at Jamestown, VA.

The image in the spyglass was fuzzy and upside down, so it wasn't very useful. But Galileo quickly improved it. The instrument he created, called a telescope, allowed him to see much more in the sky. Soon he was making telescopes and selling them throughout Europe.

> Soon Galileo was making telescopes and selling them throughout Europe.

One clear night, Galileo climbed a tower and turned his best telescope toward the sky. Everywhere he looked, he saw things no one had ever seen before. He saw that the moon had craters, mountains, and valleys. He saw that the Milky Way was really made of countless stars. Galileo was astounded!

Then in 1610, Galileo made his greatest discovery with the telescope. While observing the planet Jupiter, he noticed it was in line with three points of light that seemed to be stars. Two of the points were on one side of the planet and one was on the other side. The next night, all three stars were on the same side of Jupiter. What was going on?

The *Voyager 1* space probe took this picture of the planet Jupiter. The small round objects are two of Jupiter's moons—Io and Europa—which were both discovered by Galileo.

Europa

Io

Galileo and his son, Vincenzo

Galileo eagerly awaited his nightly viewing. Sometimes there were only two stars. Sometimes there were four. The pattern kept changing. There was only one explanation. These stars were orbiting Jupiter. When he couldn't see some of them, they were behind the planet. Galileo had discovered Jupiter's four largest moons.

Old Enemies Read a New Book

Galileo's discovery about Jupiter was just the proof he needed. Ptolemy and the Church said that all heavenly bodies circle Earth. But here were four heavenly bodies circling Jupiter. Surely, here was proof of Copernicus's idea that the planets could circle the sun.

Galileo put his thoughts to paper and wrote a book called *The Starry Messenger,* which included his observations. The book was popular...and that was a problem.

1611
King James Version of the Bible is published

1616
William Shakespeare dies.

1621
First American Thanksgiving feast celebrated in Plymouth Colony

Many of Galileo's old enemies were jealous and still did not believe him. His ideas alarmed Church leaders. Galileo accepted a new job in Florence in the Republic of Tuscany. His friends warned him not to go. The Church had even greater power in Florence than in Padua. But Galileo longed to return to the land of his youth. Besides, he looked forward to showing the Church that he was right.

Proving Them Wrong

Trouble started soon after Galileo arrived in Florence. A powerful priest in Rome condemned the teachings of Galileo and Copernicus. Galileo went to Rome to talk to Church leaders, but he never had a chance. He was warned that he must not defend Copernicus's model of the universe.

While in Florence, Galileo obeyed the Church's warning— at least in public. Although he kept working on other problems of motion, he longed to write a book. It would compare Ptolemy's and Copernicus's models of the universe. Galileo wanted to show the world once and for all that Copernicus was right.

> Galileo wanted to show the world once and for all that Copernicus was right.

1630

Johannes Kepler dies.

1632

Galileo's *Dialogue* published

In 1623, Galileo's hopes rose. A good friend of his had become the pope, the leader of the Catholic Church. Years before, this man had appreciated Galileo's experiments. He had seemed open to new ideas. Galileo went back to Rome to seek permission to write his book from the head of the Church himself.

The pope granted permission with two conditions. First, Copernicus's model must be presented only as an idea, not as a fact. Second, the Church must approve the book before it was printed. Galileo happily agreed.

Galileo called his book *Dialogue Concerning the Two Chief World Systems,* or the *Dialogue* for short. It was written as a conversation among three people. One character took the viewpoint of Copernicus and Galileo. Another character, named Simplicio (meaning, in Latin, "simple-minded"), took the viewpoint of Ptolemy. The third character was named Sagredo.

The Inquisition ordered Galileo to stand trial in Rome.

In the book, Sagredo was an open-minded person who would decide which model of the universe was correct. The book presented all arguments for and against each model. But in the end, the reader was left with no doubt. Copernicus's model was correct. Despite this ending, the Church granted Galileo permission to publish the book.

The Inquisition Bears Down

As with Galileo's earlier book, the *Dialogue* became popular. But once again trouble started. Some people said that Galileo used the pope as the model for Simplicio, the simple-minded character. They said that Galileo was making fun of the pope.

The pope was furious. The Church banned the *Dialogue*. No copies of the book would be sold. The Inquisition ordered Galileo to come to Rome and stand trial for heresy.

> After his sentence,
> Galileo was banned from
> writing for the public.

The trial went badly for Galileo, and the Inquisition found him guilty. He was held in prison to await an unknown sentence. If Galileo held firm to his beliefs, he might be tortured—placed on a rack and stretched until he was severely injured. He was now 69 years old, and that kind of torture could kill him. Some heretics were burned at the stake. Friends told him to save himself by doing whatever the Inquisitors asked.

On June 22, 1633, Galileo was brought before the court to hear his sentence—life imprisonment. But first he had to write a document for the public. It had to say that all he knew about how the stars and planets move was untrue. He was greatly humiliated.

House Arrest

Galileo's imprisonment was not that bad. He was under house arrest, which meant he could not leave his home and gardens in Florence. He lived there for eight more years until his death in 1642. During that time, he did much more work explaining how things move.

As part of his sentence, Galileo was banned from writing for the public. But a friend smuggled out a book that summarized his life's work on how forces move objects. In just a few short years, this work would be carried on. The man who would continue Galileo's work was perhaps the greatest scientist the world has ever known.

The *Dialogue*

The first copy of Galileo's *Dialogue Concerning the Two Chief World Systems* came off the printing press in Florence in February 1632. It went on to become one of the most important scientific books ever written and is still studied today.

Despite this great success, things didn't start off too well for Galileo's masterpiece. When the book was first published and the negative criticism started rolling in, the book was put on the *Index Librorum Prohibitorum* (List of Prohibited Books). The Church created this list to ban certain "immoral" books from being read by its followers. Galileo's *Dialogue* remained on the list until 1822. Today, editions of *Dialogue* can be found in many languages as a tool for scientists around the world.

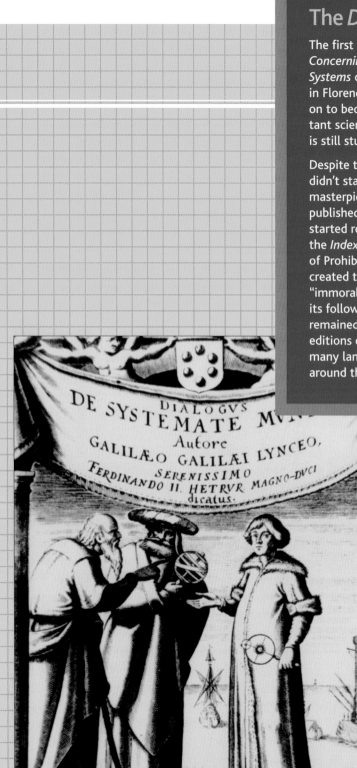

Newton attended Cambridge University in England.

ON THE SHOULDERS OF GIANTS

It's 1665, and a Great Plague is sweeping across England. Thousands of people are dying, and no one knows why. People flee the cities. Cambridge University closes and sends students home. One of these students is a young man named Isaac Newton.

Isaac Newton

BORN December 25, 1642
Woolsthorpe, Lincolnshire,
England

DIED March 20, 1727
London, England

Born in 1642, the year that Galileo died, Newton picked up right where Galileo left off. He took up the study of the universe and its principles.

At three years old, Isaac's mother, a widow, left him to be raised by his grandmother. He was often sick as a child and spent a great deal of time alone. He liked to read, build toys, and keep a journal.

At the age of 19, Isaac headed off to Cambridge University for a college education.

In 1665, he received his degree.

When the Great Plague swept through England, the university closed for two years, and Newton returned home. He had many scientific ideas he still wanted to pursue.

During his "Miraculous Year," from 1665 to 1666, Newton changed science forever. Before his 25th birthday, Newton had invented calculus, examined how planets move, developed many laws of physics, and discovered the law of universal gravitation, among other accomplishments.

Newton also discovered the theory of optics. He was the first person to realize that white light is made up of the colors of the rainbow.

In 1687 he published the famed *Principia (Principles)*. Much of the book was about his law of gravity, but the book also contained his three laws of motion. A physicist and mathematician, Isaac was knighted in 1705, becoming Sir Isaac Newton.

1642

Galileo Galilei dies.

Isaac Newton is born.

1665

The Great Plague hits Europe.

1665

Jan Vermeer paints
Girl with a Pearl Earring.

In the safe, peaceful setting of his country home, Isaac Newton could concentrate. In 1665 and 1666, during his "Miraculous Year," he thought of some of the most important ideas in science.

By then, science had made some progress because of Copernicus, Galileo, and others, but progress was slow. Many educated people still believed in witchcraft. Events such as storms and earthquakes were blamed on spirits. Sick people were made to bleed to get rid of their "bad blood."

People still had trouble accepting the idea of a moving Earth. "If the Earth spins," they said, "why don't things fly off into space?" No one had a good answer. Galileo had shown how many things move, but he had not said why they move that way. Newton would answer this question.

Invisible Force?

In 1666, Newton discovered gravity, an invisible force that affects objects in space. The idea was very hard for people to imagine. By now, however, most scientists had accepted the idea that the planets orbit the sun. Johannes Kepler, a German astronomer of Galileo's time, helped prove this idea.

The moon, which orbits Earth, is shown above Earth's horizon.

1666

Newton spots the famous
falling apple.

1666

The Great Fire of London destroys
80 percent of the city.

Johannes Kepler

BORN December 27, 1571
Weil der Stadt, Wiirttemberg

DIED November 15, 1630
Imperial Free City of
Regensburg

Kepler, a German astronomer
and mathematician, lived
at the same time as Galileo.
Johannes was born into a
Protestant family. He was
often sick as a child, but man-
aged to study hard and
attend good schools.

Johannes's work paid off and
in 1589 he earned a scholar-
ship to the University of
Tubingen. There he had professors who accepted the
Copernican model of the
universe. He took a job as
a math teacher in Austria,
where his great love of
astronomy blossomed.
Johannes collected precise
data on the planets and their
movements. He used his data
to propose three laws of
planetary motion. Kepler's
laws later helped Isaac
Newton explain gravity.

Kepler showed that the orbits of the planets were ellipses,
or ovals. They were not perfect circles. Further, Kepler
showed that the planets move faster in their orbits as they
get closer to the sun. He didn't know why the speed
changes, just that it does. Kepler spoke about a "planet-
moving force."

That planet-moving force is gravity. Newton thought
about how apples fall, and he realized that the force that
pulled the apple to the ground is not limited just to Earth.
He used math to prove that gravity pulls any two objects
together, no matter what they are or where they are in the
universe. Gravity is the force that keeps the moon and
planets in their orbits.

How Gravity Works

Both Earth and the apple pull on each other. Why doesn't
Earth rise up to the apple, or at least meet it halfway? The
more mass, or matter, an object has, the more it pulls on
other objects. Earth has a lot more mass than the apple.
Therefore, Earth's pull is greater, and the apple moves
toward it.

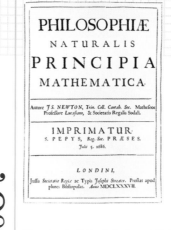

1687 Newton's *Principia* is published.

Earth and the moon also pull on each other. Earth has more mass than the moon, so Earth pulls the moon toward it. Then why doesn't the moon fall to Earth? Newton thought about this question. Then he remembered a game he used to play. A child would hold a rope tied to a bucket of water. The object of the game was to twirl the bucket around and around without spilling the water. If you could twirl the bucket quickly enough, you wouldn't lose a drop. Suddenly Newton understood why the moon doesn't fall to Earth.

The moon is constantly falling to Earth. But the moon also has a sideways motion. The combination of the sideways motion and Earth's gravity pulls the moon into an orbit. Similarly, the sun's gravity holds the planets in their orbits. The force of gravity gets weaker the farther two objects are from each other. Pluto is the planet farthest from the sun. So the gravity that holds Pluto in its orbit is weaker than the gravity that holds Earth in its orbit.

Newton's idea of gravity was proved so often that it became known as a law—the law of gravity. It's what keeps objects, and people, from flying off Earth. Gravity pulls us to Earth and keeps us grounded.

Putting a Bucket in Orbit

You can demonstrate how planets orbit the sun. Tie a rope to a bucket handle and fill the bucket with water. The water-filled bucket represents the Earth. You represent the sun. Hold onto the rope and twirl the bucket around. You'll notice that you don't get wet; that's because the bucket is being pulled toward you by force, as if it is orbiting around you. The rope represents gravity. When you twirl the bucket, you're adding sideways motion to the bucket of water.

If you let go of the rope, the bucket would fly off into the air in a staight line. By letting go, you've broken the force holding the bucket and you together.

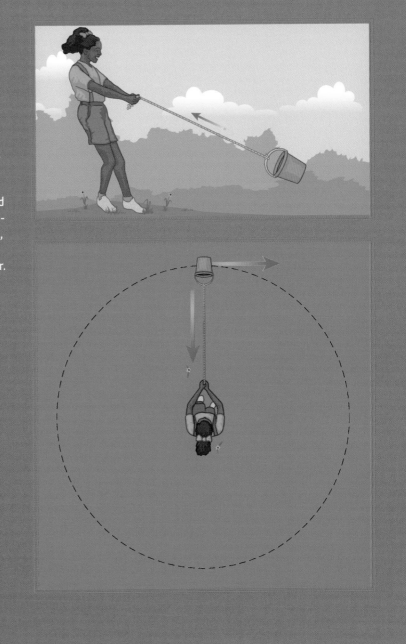

A painting depicting 17th-century London

NEWTON'S MASTERPIECE

4

Isaac Newton was strange in some ways. As brilliant as he was, and as careful as he was, he didn't like to let other people see his work. He didn't like criticism. It was 20 years before he told the world about his biggest ideas on gravity and motion. And he had to be convinced to do it even then.

1727

Isaac Newton dies.

1700

English population in the American colonies reaches 250,000.

Isaac Newton belonged to a group of English scientists called the Royal Society. For the most part, discussions among members were good exchanges. But Newton and another member, Robert Hooke, seldom agreed on anything.

Hooke was well respected. He invented a kind of microscope. He was the first to use the word "cell" to describe the building blocks of living things. But Hooke seemed to be jealous of Newton. Sometimes he claimed Newton's ideas as his own.

Newton had worked out most of his own ideas of motion during the Great Plague of 1665–1666. But Hooke claimed that some of the ideas were his. In 1684, Newton had a visit from his best friend, the scientist Edmund Halley. Halley wanted Newton to publish his ideas on motion to make sure Newton got credit for them.

> Newton had worked out most of his own ideas of motion during the Great Plague of 1665–1666.

Newton's friend Edmund Halley was an English astronomer and mathematician who in 1682 discovered the most famous of all comets—Halley's Comet.

While studying the paths of comets seen between 1337 and 1698, Halley showed that one comet had actually returned three times during this period. Then he predicted its return in 1758. Halley's discovery proved that some comets are members of the solar system. Halley's Comet orbits the sun every 75–76 years. It was last seen in 1986 and can be expected to be visible again in 2062.

This bobsled rushes down the track at a steady speed, illustrating the first law of motion.

Newton agreed. He spent 20 months working day and night to complete his book. He fully explained his great discoveries about motion and gravity. He finished his masterpiece in April 1687. It was called *Philosophiae Naturalis Principia Mathematica,* or *Principia (Principles)*. Much of the book was about his law of gravity. It also included what became known as Newton's three laws of motion.

Many scientists call *Principia* the greatest book of science ever written. With just a few simple laws, Newton helped people understand why things move as they do. He also gave people the power to predict how things will move.

First Law of Motion

Newton's first law of motion picks up on a thought that Galileo had. Galileo pointed out that an object could be set in motion with just the slightest force—a push or a pull. If nothing slows it down, a rolling ball on a level surface could roll forever. No extra force would be needed to keep the ball moving.

The force of the bat striking the ball causes the ball to accelerate.

The first law of motion says that an object that is at rest, or not moving, will stay at rest unless a force acts on it. For example, a bobsled stays still until it's pushed or pulled. The first law also says that an object that is moving will move at the same speed and in the same direction unless a force acts on it. A sliding bobsled keeps sliding until someone puts on the brakes. This idea of how rest or motion will stay the same is called inertia.

Second Law of Motion

Newton's second law of motion says that an object accelerates because a force acts on it. To accelerate means to change speed or direction or both. The stronger the force, the more the object accelerates.

1781

Steam engine developed to
power machines

Also, the more mass an object has, the more force is needed to change its motion. Which is harder to push, a real
car or a toy car? The real car is harder to push because it
has more mass.

Third Law of Motion

Newton's third law of motion says that for every action,
there is an equal and opposite reaction. Usually, more
than one force acts on an object at a time. And usually
more than one of Newton's laws of motion applies to any
movement. The canoe in the opposite photo shows all of
Newton's laws of motion in action. Newton's first law says
that the canoe will stay still until a force moves it. This
force comes from the push of the paddles.

> Usually, more
> than one force
> acts on an object
> at a time.

Newton's second law explains how the canoe changes speed or direction or both. The people and equipment give the canoe a lot of mass. When the paddlers want to change the canoe's acceleration, they have to paddle with a lot of force.

Newton's third law explains why the paddling works in the first place. With each stroke, a paddler pushes water backward—an action. This backward force produces an equal and opposite force—a reaction—that moves the canoe forward.

The weight of the canoers and the amount of energy they use to paddle determine how fast the canoe will move.

Newton's work paved the way for the industrial revolution beginning in the 1700s. Machines filled factories, and steam engines powered ships and railroads. All of these inventions came from applying Newton's laws of motion.

FROM NEWTON TO SPACEFLIGHT

It didn't take long for people to start using Newton's laws of motion. They made better clocks, better waterwheels, and many other things with moving parts. By applying the laws of motion, engineers could usually tell if a machine would work before it was built. Newton had changed the world.

Newton's laws of motion have made an impact on much of the technology used in modern-day life.

Cars, rockets, bicycles—these are just a few of the inventions that use Newton's laws of motion. Almost every mechanical invention since Newton's time has depended on his laws.

Even some objects that don't move, like huge suspension bridges and skyscrapers, demonstrate the principle of inertia. How do you keep an object from starting to move? According to Newton's first law, one answer would be to keep a force from acting on the object.

Newton's work paved the way for the industrial revolution beginning in the 1700s. Machines filled factories, and steam engines powered ships and railroads. All these inventions came from applying Newton's laws of motion.

Exploring Space

Newton's laws of motion and gravity have helped us explore space. A rocket uses all the laws to get into space. Hot gases shoot backward and push the rocket forward.

1788

1789 First nationwide election held in the United States

The U.S. Constitution is ratified.

While moving, the rocket can change directions by shooting off gas in one direction, which sends the rocket in the opposite direction. Without Newton, we would not know how to send satellites into orbit around Earth. Many of our televisions and phones, which depend on satellites, would not work as they do.

The Courage of New Ideas

Nicolaus Copernicus bravely disagreed with old ideas about the world. Galileo Galilei proposed new ideas to replace the old ones. Even though the Church stopped Galileo from sharing his ideas, Isaac Newton found out about them. Newton studied Galileo's experiments and Kepler's ideas. Newton experimented on objects in motion. He stated new laws of science that replaced many of the old ideas.

Newton once said, "If I have seen farther, it is by standing on the shoulders of giants." These scientists were giants not only because of their ideas. They were also giants because they had the courage to express new ideas during dangerous times.

> Almost every mechanical invention since Newton's time has depended on his laws of motion.

Ice skating uses Newton's laws of motion.

GLOSSARY

Accelerate
change speed, direction, or both

Arc
curved line

Astrolabe
an instrument used to measure the position of stars and planets

Astronomy
study of matter outside Earth's atmosphere

Ellipses
oval shapes

Force
a push or a pull

Gravity
force of attraction between any two objects

Heretic
a person who disagrees with Church teachings

Inertia
property of matter in which an object stays at rest or in motion unless acted on by a force

Inquisition
former Roman Catholic court for putting heretics on trial

Laws of Motion
Isaac Newton's three rules for how and why things move

Mass
amount of matter in a substance

Orbit
path of one object circling another object

Pendulum
hanging object that is allowed to swing freely

Philosopher
person who seeks knowledge; in the Renaissance, a person who studied science

Rotation
turning around a center point or a straight line

Telescope
instrument for viewing distant objects through a lens

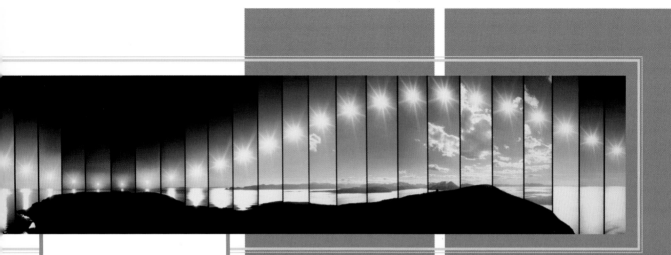

Taken in Loppa, Norway, between July 21 at 7:00 P.M. and July 22 at 6:00 P.M., this time-lapse photography shows part of the sun's cycle north of the Arctic Circle.

Biographical Resources

For more information on Nicolaus Copernicus and his scientific discoveries, go to the World Almanac for Kids at http://www.worldalmanac forkids.com/explore/space/copernicus.html.

An incredible resource on Galileo Galilei can be found at The Galileo Project web site at http://galileo.rice.edu/galileo.html.

Take the Galileo Astronomy Tour at http://www.thursdays classroom.com/03feb00/astronomytour.html.

Discover more on Isaac Newton by visiting Energy Kid's Place on the Energy Information Administration web site at http://www.eia.doe.gov/kids/history/people/pioneers.html#Newton.

Another great resource on Newton can be found at The Newton Project's web site at http://www.newtonproject.ic.ac.uk/.

There is a lot that is known about Johannes Kepler's childhood, as he wrote detailed descriptions of it in his autobiography and other writings. Find out more about him on the NASA web site at http://www.kepler.nasa.gov/johannes or on the Galileo Project web site at http://galileo.rice.edu/sci/kepler.html.

More science stuff about physics and the laws of motion

To learn more about Newton's laws of motion, check out The Physics Classroom at http://www.glenbrook.k12.il.us/gbssci/phys/class//newt-laws/newtltoc.

Having trouble understanding the laws of gravity? Try this web site for more information: http://csep10.phys.utk.edu/astr161/lect/history/newtongrav.html.

Learn how things fly by viewing an exhibition at the National Air and Space Museum at http://www.nasm.si.edu/galleries/gal109/NEWHTF/HTF030.HTM.

Other cool science stuff about space and astronomy

For all sorts of cool information on the science of astronomy, check out http://www.kidsastronomy.com.

Want to know what the stars in the sky will look like tonight? Or, do you want to send an astronomy postcard to a friend? Check out Astronomy for Kids at http://www.dustbunny.com/afk/.

NASA has put together a fun web site where you can learn all about the solar system and the universe. Take a look at StarChild at http://starchild.gsfc.nasa.gov.

What more can I do?

Check out how physics affects sports at the Exploratorium at http://www.exploratorium.edu/sports, where you can do hands-on acitivities.

Play a game! Shoot a cannonball into orbit at http://www.spaceplace.nasa.gov/en/kids/orbits1.shtml.

Care to launch a "rocket" from a spinning "planet"? Check out http://www.spaceplace.nasa.gov/en/kids/ds1_mgr.shtml.

Still have questions? Go to the U.S. Department of Energy's "Ask A Scientist" web page at http://www.newton.dep.anl.gov/aas.htm.

Also, try heading out to your local science museum or library for more information and fun facts.

INDEX

Large parts of this book were previously
published as *Defining the Laws of Motion*
(National Geographic Reading
Expeditions), copyright © 2003.

Book design by KINETIK. The body
text of the book is set in Bliss Regular.
The display text is set in Filosofia.

Library of Congress
Cataloging-in-Publication Data

Phelan, Glen.
Invisible force : the quest to define
the laws of motion / by Glen Phelan.
p. cm. — (Science quest)
Includes bibliographical references and
index.
Trade ISBN 10: 0-7922-5539-9
Trade ISBN 13: 978-0-7922-5539-0
Library ISBN 10: 0-7922-5540-2
Library ISBN 13: 978-0-7922-5540-6
1. Motion--History--Juvenile literature.
I. Title. II. Science quest (National
Geographic Society (U.S.))
QR133.5.P54 2006
531'.112 — dc22

2005027350

PUBLISHED BY THE
NATIONAL GEOGRAPHIC SOCIETY

John M. Fahey, Jr.,
President and Chief Executive Officer

Gilbert M. Grosvenor,
Chairman of the Board

Nina D. Hoffman,
*Executive Vice President, President, Book
Publishing Group*

PREPARED BY NATIONAL GEOGRAPHIC
CHILDREN'S BOOKS

Nancy Laties Feresten, *Vice President,
Editor-in-Chief of Children's Books*

Bea Jackson, *Director of Illustration and
Design, Children's Books*

Jim Hiscott, *Art Director, Children's Books
& Education Publishing Group*

Susan Kehnemui Donnelly, Priyanka
Lamichhane, *Project Editors*

KINETIK, *Designer*

Lori Epstein, *Illustrations Editor*

Jean Cantu, *Illustrations Coordinator*

Debbie Guthrie Haer, *Copy Editor*

Rebecca Hinds, *Managing Editor*

R. Gary Colbert, *Production Director*

Lewis R. Bassford, *Production Manager*

Vincent P. Ryan, *Manufacturing Manager*

Maryclare Tracy, *Manufacturing Manager*

PROGRAM DEVELOPMENT FOR
NATIONAL GEOGRAPHIC READING
EXPEDITIONS
Kate Boehm Jerome

CONSULTANT/REVIEWERS
Dr. James Shymansky, E. Desmond
Lee Professor of Science Education,
University of Missouri-St. Louis

Photo credits-Cover, © Corbis; 4-5, ©
W.Perry Conway/Corbis; 6, © Philip
James Corwin/Corbis; 8-9, ©
Bettmann/Corbis; 10, Stapleton
Collection/Corbis; 11, © Corbis; 12-13, ©
Corbis; 14 (l), © Paul Almasy/Corbis; (r),
© Bernard and Catherine Desjeux/Corbis;
15, © Bettmann/Corbis; 16, © Blue
Lantern Studio/Corbis; 17, © Paul
Almasy/Corbis; 18, © Stefano
Bianchetti/Corbis; 19, ©
Bettmann/Corbis; 20-21, Palazzo Vecchio
(Palazzo della Signoria) Florence,
Italy/Bridgeman Art Library; 22, ©
Bettmann/Corbis; 23 (l), © Istituto e
Museo di Storia della Scienza; (r) ©
Réunion des Musées Nationaux/Art
Resource, NY; 24, © Corbis; 25, © Archivo
Iconografico, S.A./Corbis; 26, North Wind
Picture Archives; 27, © Corbis; 28, ©
Scala/Art Resource, NY; 29, ©
Bettmann/Corbis; 30, © Erich
Lessing/Art Resource, NY; 31, Private
Collection/Bridgeman Art Library; 33,
Science Photo Library/Photo Researchers,
Inc.; 34-35, John Lawrence/Getty Images;
36, © Giraudon/Art Resource, NY; 37,
Painting by Jan Vermeer, photo © Francis
G. Mayer/Corbis; 38, © Corbis; 39,
Science Photo Library/Photo Researchers,
Inc.; 40, Science Photo Library/Photo
Researchers, Inc.; 41, Precision Graphics;
42-43, © Victoria & Albert Museum,
London/Art Resource, NY; 44, Photo ©
Leonard de Selva/Corbis; 45, © Roger
Ressmeyer/Corbis; 46, © Royalty
Free/Corbis; 47, © Royalty-Free/Corbis; 48,
© Gordon Osmundson/Corbis; 49, ©
Richard Hamilton Smith/Corbis; 50-51,
Harper's Weekly; 52, © Nik Wheeler
/Corbis; 53, © Peggy & Ronald Barnett
/Corbis; 54-55, © Bradley Smith/Corbis;
56, © Arnulf Husmo/Getty Images.

One of the world's largest nonprofit scientific and educational organizations, the National Geographic Society was founded in 1888 "for the increase and diffusion of geographic knowledge." Fulfilling this mission, the Society educates and inspires millions every day through its magazines, books, television programs, videos, maps and atlases, research grants, the National Geographic Bee, teacher workshops, and innovative classroom materials. The Society is supported through membership dues, charitable gifts, and income from the sale of its educational products. This support is vital to National Geographic's mission to increase global understanding and promote conservation of our planet through exploration, research, and education.

For more information, please call

1-800-NGS-LINE (647-5463)
or write to the following address:

NATIONAL GEOGRAPHIC SOCIETY
1145 17th Street N.W.
Washington, D.C. 20036-4688
U.S.A.

For information about special discounts for bulk purchases, please contact National Geographic Books Special Sales:
ngspecsales@ngs.org

Visit the Society's Web site:
www.nationalgeographic.com

Printed in Belgium.